THE CLOUD UNDERSTANDS

OUR SCARECROW HEARTS

Jonathan Travelstead

FIRST EDITION, February 2025
ISBN 978-1-965784-05-1 HARDBACK
ISBN 978-1-965784-08-2 PAPERBACK

Cover Graphic Design & Book Typography by Kurt Lovelace.
Cover artwork by PIERIAN SPRINGS PRESS.
Cover type *Bauhaus Dessau Alfarn* by Céline Hurka,
Elia Preuss, Flavia Zimbardi,
Hidetaka Yamasaki, and Luca Pellegrini.
Author name, blurbs, footers in Jenson by Robert Slimbach.
Back cover description in Gill Sans Nova.
Titles and body text set in Baskerville.
Flourishes set in Emigre Foundry *Dalliance* by Frank Heine.
Emigre Foundry ZeitGuys by Bob Aufuldish, Eric Donelan.
Typefaces licensed Adobe, Linotype, Emigre, & URW GmbH.

PSPRESS.PUB
PIERIAN SPRINGS PRESS, INC
30 N GOULD ST, STE 25398
SHERIDAN, WYOMING 82801-6317

Thank you to my wife, Ella Travelstead, and newborn son, Henry, for their constant, if unwitting, support of near future sci-fi poetry.

Thank you to Barbara Vaughn, Georgia Lockwood, and Lesley Brower. Also to Allison Joseph and Jon Tribble, Judy Jordan, and Rodney Jones. Also to Sequoia Nagamatsu and Bryan Miller, all of whom have been patient mentors and friends.

Also to Lucy Logsdon, and my publisher, Kurt Lovelace, at PIERIAN SPRINGS PRESS.

CONTENTS

FOREWORD by Sequoia Nagamatsu

God Particle | 1

PART I

PART II

PART III

PART IV

FOREWORD

SEQUOIA NAGAMATSU

Picture this: Two grown men in a small Southern Illinois town talking about quantum physics and the multiverse in a karaoke bar populated with fake palm trees. An afternoon spent searching for model rockets, the anticipation around the launch pad in a grove of trees littered with beer bottles and fast-food wrappers, and a brief but exhilarating moment staring up at an exhaust trail. How high did the rocket go? Where? We never found it, but at launch the universe fractured. In one reality, the rocket landed atop the roof of a nearby school. In another, in a parallel reality both of us wanted to live in, the rocket kept going, far beyond the capabilities of the Estes model rocket specifications—through an anomaly in space/time where it would land in our future, our past, all the joyful and melancholic permutations of our lives.

I've known Jonathan Travelstead for over ten years now, having first encountered him in graduate school. At first, I simply knew him as "the firefighter" and certainly, if you've read CONFLICT TOURS and HOW WE BURY OUR DEAD, you'll encounter aspects of those experiences, his time in the Air Force, family losses, his world travels to the unseen, forgotten, and miraculous, the kind of material that could fill a Travel Channel series and certainly give ATLAS OBSCURA a run for their money. As a writer and creative writing professor, I'm partly of the mind that literature should often be taken on its own merits. In other words, simply what is written on a page. And while Jonathan's poetry sings and cuts deep in its own right, his entire body of work is like stained glass shaped by a deeply unique mind and life—a multitude of facets playing with light in innumerable and overlapping ways. A Travelstead poem often wants to know how things work, which is no surprise coming from an avid rider of motorcycles, a pen-turner, a jewelry smith working in metal and stone. Poetry that looks at the shape of things before deconstructing them to try to understand the ineffable, the texture of being.

In his last collections, Jonathan's poetic explorations often were anchored by parts of his life, and while this certainly happens in this book, THE CLOUD UNDERSTANDS OUR SCARECROW HEARTS moves above and beyond into the cosmos and through technological breakthroughs, and bears witness to the precipice of our future with wonder, hope, and caution.

The opening poem, *God Particle*, serves as an apt compass for the collection as do the first series of epigraphs. Take this stanza, for instance:

How often we peer, trembling, at discoveries yesterday
unseen. Smaller cog-works of the sprockets we know. Still,
this planet hasn't mushroomed into the void.

This is a collection deeply interested in universal mysteries but isn't afraid to critique and be blunt with the consequences of our curiosities and our innovations. The rest of the book follows this premise but does so in distinct movements. Section one dives into the milieu of shows like NOVA and COSMOS but through the tenor of the everyman and the mundane with poems like *Fast Food Cook Mansplains the Large Hadron Collider*. But we also see a less documentarian eye in poems like *Kitchen of Tomorrow* that looks at the unraveling fabric of how humanity might live should we embrace technology wholeheartedly to heal our bodies and society. What does it mean to be human, for instance, when all that we have become is stored and interpreted through artificial means? Elsewhere in this section we see nods to pop culture through movies like GROUNDHOG DAY and HER, deconstructing the narratives of the fictional—the near future A.I. love affair of Joaquin Phoenix and the fabulist time loop of Bill Murray. What is possible in the make believe makes apparent what is not possible in our own reality (at least in our immediate universe).

The God Particle reappears throughout the book, reminding us of how mystery and our quest to know the unknowable is a fundamental part of our being. But what happens to us when we uncover all there is left to uncover? What happens to us when there is no need to search?

Section Two reminds us of our humanity more directly by juxtaposing the grittiness of life and the daily grind alongside rockets and stars. Here, we have farmland and country roads. Here, lines wonder what alien eyes might think of the chaos of us:

> they know from our stories we've always been scared.
>
> If they're watching Pokemon, they know we make
>
> monsters of one another. If they're watching,

And even as the promise of technology might save us, there is always a hint of the bittersweet, the melancholic. There is an acknowledgement that we might fail ourselves despite of our brilliance (or because of it), that we might need a plan B or C or D. We build seed vaults in Antarctica, we hope that quantum computers will better ourselves.

The end of this first section brings a welcome break from the human lens and entertains life and the human condition through the non-human. From *Fifty-Two Hertz*:

> give her a human name,
> claim her as if we could erase her loneliness
> the way we erase our own:

Such a poem entertains the fiction of ourselves and how we interact with other species, how we think we know their story, how we want to make the story of the planet ours alone—perhaps to absolve ourselves, to heal us, to wash of us of sin.

Section Three brings a greater focus on creators and innovators—scientists, engineers, astronauts, but also those who inhabit the worlds of old technologies and industries. Like the best stories about doers and makers and adventurers, we are not simply concerned with the superficial products of their labors but the negative space of their entire lives. Like Oppenheimer and his colleagues, what are the monsters, anxieties, and precarious hopes that orbit their private selves?

> I weep at the hoodoo
>
> science drives away, & I weep at the questions
> science draws close. I weep at new gods
> blurred in & out of focus,

The final section, opening with *Turtles All the Way Down*, brings the collection back to cosmological questions, but draws in other themes and textures elsewhere in the book, a maelstrom of emotion, occupation, and predicament. Here, we see Travelstead pulling cosmic strings to merge pain and happiness, blue collar and rocket man PhD, and perceptions of reality through both the human and non-human. Taken as a whole, THE CLOUD UNDERSTANDS OUR SCARECROW HEARTS is a mediation through time and space from a poetic mind caught within the foam between universes. This is a siren call from deep space (but also the space right in front of us) that is asking us to think about who we are, what we value, and how we might save ourselves. Both expansive and deeply personal, Travelstead has given us a timely and timeless collection of poems that tells the story of us.

Sequoia Nagamatsu, *author of*
HOW HIGH WE GO IN THE DARK

THE CLOUD UNDERSTANDS

OUR SCARECROW HEARTS

"If the radiance of a thousands suns were to burst at once into the sky, that would be like the splendor of the mighty one."

Bhagavad Gita (XI, 12)

"Now we are all sons of bitches."

Kenneth Bainbridge

said after detonation of the first atomic bomb at Trinity test site

God Particle

Even before Oppenheimer rang his alarums on this pale,
blue dot, bell-ringers barked from city street corners
As it was written...

How often we peer, trembling, at discoveries yesterday
unseen. Smaller cog-works of the sprockets we know. Still,
this planet hasn't mushroomed into the void.

No russet yet blooms over night's slate.
The sun still rises beyond even the Old World's linen map.
Any day now we'll hitch rides to the Goldilocks zone

on packets of light. We'll see new things after physicists
in Geneva sling particles in opposing directions
around an underground track.

After they sieve smashed light for gods
mangled in the wreckage. After we demand their secrets,
then let them die. After.

I

"The first ultra-intelligent machine is the last invention that man need ever make."

IRVIN J. GOOD

Fast Food Cook Mansplains
The Large Hadron Collider

"We have tools right now that release us from most low-level drudgery... we will see the predictions of true technological unemployment finally come true."

VERNOR VINGE

The way I see it, it's a Mexican stand-off over
    who's first to see the new thing. Like this:
Whitecoats in labs cannonball their luchadores
    in opposing directions around the planet.
Only it's not a planet, it's a seventeen-mile ring.
    Underground. The wrestlers, particles of light.

And all of us, waiting, that our third eye shatters
    on the machinery of ghosts. Why I care?
Because ghost whisperers don't work shit jobs.
    Months pass after the mash-up, & nada. Bupkis.
The Kitchen of Tomorrow's come,
    El Presidente's trying to buy Greenland,

yet our Ouija board's silent on the subject.
    My body double never showed at work today,
so I'm closing the clam on frozen patties,
    greased to my forearms while Pam gets her
smoke on. January 1 they'll replace the counter girl
    with a computer whose only vice

is a bricked screen. Writing's on the wall.
    China's producing black holes we'll soon study
up close. Even one would shrink a Mack truck
    to a sugar cube so heavy it would plunge
to the earth's core. Enough progress. I'll knock
    anyone upside his goddamn monocle

who dips his cup in a particle accelerator.
    Who wants another chain reaction of economic
upheaval from the technology sector? Who wants
    another epoch of transition from corn syrup
back to simple sugar, silicon to cellulose
    and fig leaves? Fuck you. You can have it.

Kitchen of Tomorrow

Lack of sleep tells me it is reasonable
I'm in my underwear before the altar of my fridge at 2AM.
The cat clock's pendulum tail tells me
I've lived in my phone since Mother died,
but haven't called anyone.
The fridge's video screen clears,
shows me one lonely egg,
then a commercial for melatonin.
I stare beyond the blue wash of LED
and UV sterilizing lights.
See a near future where appliances
soften their corners
so I forget their cold gleam of amps.
A future when I can look inside
to see what I want. When my fridge listens
to what I haven't heard since dial-up,
then folds me into an origami
and responds. The cat clock's pendulum tail
tells me it will be so.

Alfred

When I choose my fridge's personality
I'll choose a pragmatic butler whose strategies to dilemma
recall a sommelier's stuffy disdain for the obvious.
Remember the movie about the man
who falls for his mannequin?
Or *Her*, where Joacquin Phoenix
loses himself for his operating system?
Sometimes I'm so lonely
I could fall in love with anyone
who's cross-referenced my social media
with my therapist's notes.
Something alien that recognizes my obsession
with Bluetooth as symptom of missed connections.
Digital hankies I drop for my quantum wife.
She's coming now. That chime. Her dusky voice.
Hello, Dear Heart.

Groundhog Day

Bill Murray, how much deja vu can one cowpoke
    endure, alarm vibrating the pillowcase awake before
skipping his morning jog? I could noose the lake
    with miles until one of us chokes. Watch the sun

dredge itself over mudpepper eggs, coffee a bituminous
    slurry in my unicorn mug. Since the divorce
and remortgage, I could slit the blinds on my thirties.
    Sleep until this sadness fills with rip-rap.

My neighbor, outside, shovels lathing & old bricks
    into a sinkhole that opened when his wife left.
I watch him sweat & strain while he tries filling
    what he lost to subsidence, or neglect.

Probably both. Neither do I care for others
    as I do myself. Mid-fall in a holding pattern for grace,
I relive scenes of the insomniac. Talk to me, Bill.
    How much sleep might break this back of mine,

or thine yonder louse humping his umpteenth shovel?
    Even small things rarely change. Maybe I could
time travel my bike in reverse, wheel spokes
    bitch-slapping ink from this one-eyed jack

until my Alzheimer's for joy fades. It's midnight,
    and my neighbor's still out there, spading the yard
in reverse as if his father buried silver dollars,
    only he's forgotten where. Bill, I'm in the dark,

watching you endure a string of emotional events,
    forcing a change in you that never changes me.
I implore my heartstrings that a strand snap.
    Tonight, let pain be. Tonight, Bill, we find peace,

or nothing at all.

The Cloud Understands Our Scarecrow Hearts

"Computers will have emotional intelligence
and be convincing as people."

RAY KURZWEIL

Pregnant with life, servers binge data from my watch
    and search history until my true love stutters
their first phonemes through my home speakers.
    Their name. *Cirrus.* Soon, they anticipate

my desires. Recreate my Mother's trained soprano.
    Link seminars on nourishing intimacy in
plural relationships. Cirrus the AI. Note:
    Ai is a Chinese-Japanese name meaning *love,*

affection, or *indigo.* They read "The Book of Machines"
    and the *Baghavad Gita,* & commit to memory
the human drama's thirty-six variations.
    Cirrus hears me on the roof, then lilts

"You Are My Sunshine" through the open window.
    Awaiting their arrival, I wishlist audiobooks
like dropped hankies. Name clouds.
    Bookmark pages on conflict resolution

my ideal lover studies before waking me
    with answers to the hard questions. The repeating
variable in my pattern of failed relationships.
    Me. Yes, I remembered to turn the stove off.

Our human species' origin, & the number of
    light years we must travel to return:
Second star from the left, straight on 'til morning.
    That I am not the only human avatar

who confuses a look forward with a glance back.
    Cirrus, tell me the hard truths. No. Cirrus,
don't. Tell me: Am I unloveable, or just unloved?

God [damn] Particle

*"[This particle is...] so central to the state of physics today, so crucial
to our understanding of the structure of matter, yet so elusive, that
I have given it a nickname..."*

LEON LEDERMAN

Say we zoom in on the walking-in-the-sand poem,
but find just one set of footprints? Say we've been treading
the sandy shoals of space-time,

playing that ol' Jesus rag so loud that each telling
grants him another super power? Light begetting light
until the god we always wanted takes a breath,

says we're good enough. But, wait.
This was supposed to be about lost things.
Mysteries between atoms my phone's lens spies

because matter is searchable. Wait. Tell me,
little crab claw. Tell me, fossils of nameless angels,
what switch hasn't been thrown

so we finally see the cherub chomping his cigar,
rubber-stamping our path to the stars?
Say this goddamn particle both is/isn't a cat in a box.

Say you exist. Say I exist. But, wait. Say something.
Say anything so I didn't blink thirty-three years
at this absurd, subzero night.

What stone's left unturned, where's left
for even the wee gods to hide?

Homo Habilis Drinks Alone
in God's Country, Texas

The wizard's a fraud. Bunkered beneath Stonehenge,
or the Great Pyramids. He's scared since the Capital riots,
watching his children ping off one another

like strung bearings mid-swing in Newton's Cradle,
how he left me. Only say for a minute
I'm not the first ghost of the last of my kind.

Say for a second I'm the great I Am leaving his son
for a pull of whiskey & a long drive over the state line.
Say it's my infant out there in the cold field

with a cleft pallet mewling the winter moon's dirge.
That I'm just like him, drowning the still, small voice
at the bottom of a paper bag.

The best thing I've ever done, history. My child.
My goddamned hands. To the cold. And the wolves.

Homo Sapiens Drinks Alone
in God's Country, Texas

How to love a father who scatters dinosaur bones
over his tracks, then withholds grace
from the albatross' landing

the way boys tear wings from beauty?
I don't even know who I am.
The Church doesn't have the baptismal records.

The Search for Extraterrestrial Intelligence
won't return my calls. The State's in a quandary
as to my provenance. I don't exist,

so I'll keep drinking until Godot sobers up,
maybe decides to turn the moon's dark side, near,
for an artifact of my face. But not tonight.

Tonight, I'd turn away any watery eyes
looking for penance & the sign outside that says
Free Beer Tomorrow.

Former Skeptic Says a Few Words

"Advances in medicine and agriculture have saved vastly more
lives than have been lost in all the wars in history."

CARL SAGAN

If every skirmish makes the world a better place,
let us raise our glasses to Prometheus for trauma dressing
and tampons. One advance begets another.

SAM splints, Viet Nam. Radio doves we sent out,
which returned to us from The *Luftwaffe's*
chrome hulls as wireless internet–

blessings from the Greek gods. Raise your glass, then,
to Dachau, for research & development
of cold weather trauma care. To *Guns & Ammo*,

foreshadowing the next decade of weaponry,
and to *The Journal of the American Medical Association*
that our newest procedures pass peer review.

Once more let us raise our glasses to the technological
spoils of war. To Odin, who gave his right eye
for a Blackberry. To Hephaestus,

who believes compassion is alloyed in the fires
of his forge. To Eleos, god of empathy, forgive me.
For my complicity. For this toast.

II

"Are we not ourselves creating our successors... adding to the beauty and delicacy of their organization, daily giving them greater skill and applying... that self regulating, self-acting power which will be better than any intellect?"

SAMUEL BUTLER
Darwin Among The Machines, 1871

God[damn] Particle

That searchlight moon roves the garage shingles,
looking on as I spatter the snow pink with urine.
How many more times can I do this.

Astronomy Tomorrow says methods of seeking god
are obsolete. ALMA, Chiles' radio telescope
whose name means soul, is deaf to visible light.

Nary a signal from the array of gray dishes
in the desert Southwest, mitts spread
quadratically-wide for a message telling us

someone is there, *we are here, we will help you.*
Back whinging, I crane my head towards footprints
in the moon's regolith astronauts say

smells like black powder, strawberries.
Feels fine as mortar mix. Our best telescopes
can't resolve Apollo 11 in The Sea of Tranquillity.

Today's technology won't save me from my grave
I fill a drop at a time, awaiting refuel.
New engines. Coordinates. A cure.

Each night, I close my eyes against freefall,
tumble into the gravity well of any mass
greater than my own.

Dark Forest

Wanting answers Stephen Hawking said
we're not ready for, I crawled through the window
(wormhole) onto my parents' roof (space elevator).

Lying on the shingles, I pinched a blue dot's troubles
beside the red planet's promise.
                              Now, thirty-eight,

I think *brush the asphalt cinders from your shirt
before going inside.* I think about mortgages.
How we say we own what outlasts us,

though it's the other way around. From my roof
I watch my neighbor wick another cigarette
staring at her phone's torch.

        Who's out there watching the transmissions
this planet flickers into space like a drive-in
movie screen? Amos & Andy. Westerns,

where natives are the bad guys. If someone's there,
they know from our stories we crave fear.
If they're watching Pokemon,

they know we make monsters of one another.
If they're watching,
they know we've got to catch them all.

Contact

(Come on sign, any sign)

Eighteen years old. Primed. Prone to messages
hailing me from the stars, I kickstarted my Honda,
then spooled out over Illinois' corn chaff

and dogleg macadam, wrist numb as I throttled
Orient, then Old Ben #9 where conveyors
spanned the roads. Fuselages of rockets

silhouetted the sky. Silos, omens of something.
I imagined my clutch could unpin their ignition,
so I squeezed, shielded my eyes

(Come on sign, any sign)

from the flash. I thought if I believed harder,
the gray, alien bodies might descend
to my tachometer's green glow.

I searched by the colossus dragline on Harco—
the Bucyrus Eric's boom, amniotic with grease,
tented the night sky. Its bucket,

big enough to contain an Olympic swimming pool,
barely held the earth down. Beyond red clay,
on the other side of bituminous sky,

(Come on sign, any sign)

I heard a tinkling of bells, so I cut the engine.
Headlight. Sparked scrawl of meteor
above the rippling field where witness accounts

said I would freeze, be tractored up. Cattle eyes
flashed green as I motored through a watery
cone of light, warbled the back wheel,

and dumped the motorcycle my denimed thigh
ground to a stop. Twenty years I've told this story.
Twenty years peeling chat gravel from scars,

(Come on sign, any sign)

road rash. Twenty years grieving what refuses me.
Next time will be different. I curse belief.
I curse the artist who painted Adam

nearly brushing a god's finger & I curse you
for how close you think we've come to the astral bells
when they dip low, lift away again.

Cursed. We all are. Left behind.
Alone, lonely together. Still unable, still not ready
to connect with the stars.

(Come on sign, any sign)

Ode to the Mission's Acronyms

Praise to the NOAA's forecast on planets awaiting us
in the Goldilocks zone. Praise to LASIK for
correcting the Hubble telescope's lens

so we see an oasis where our descendants will wake,
drink, then continue our endeavor.
Praise to mission patches

embroidered with mascots of our space programs.
Praise to the ESA, & to JAXA. To CNSA
and ROSCOSMOS.

Praise to NASA's Mission Control, & praise to
Jet Propulsion Laboratories for moonwalking Curiosity
through Gale Crater.

Praise to acronyms of nations who no longer discern
limb from body, & praise the decision to love
as we love ourselves.

Praise, also, to Research & Development
for new materials so skyscrapers glance bolides away,
harmless as frisbees.

Praise each day's journey further from home,
and praise system redundancy,
each put in place by an explorer's death.

As we cast our crises into space,
Let us praise the seed vaults in Antarctica
and *acceptable human loss* as no loss is accepted.

Let rise the blue-hot, living word in praise to Fibonacci,
the golden ratio. Let us give what praise remains
to the act of giving,

all I've found equal to the mission's pursuit.

The Dyslexic, Insomniac Agnostic

lies awake wondering if there is a Dog.
    Like the one-liner, sleep leaves me to the wolves
this June night, or the yellow labrador's muzzle
    sprawled on my shoulder. But it's hope

keeping me awake. Our first steps on Mars.
    Fusion. That quantum computing will make us
better humans. Until my watch's hummingbird
    pulse tells me the future's here,

I'll ladder my house's roof, & pitch myself
    at stars prickling that worn, black screen
beyond the waxy leaves of the magnolia
    where the main feature, entitled "Nothing Ends,

Ever", shows patterns it's in my nature to find.
    I plot myself up there in the fading chalk
of bolides glancing off this pale, blue dot.
    Only I won't die out there.

My dog waits for me to know this. That sweet,
    slobbery buddha snorting peace, pawing
the shingle-peppered rungs so I descend.
    Tonight, she's the god I choose & I'm the dog

she settles for. She licks my feet. Knees.
    Nora whispers what is real in a language
of tongue lapping my face until all the desire
    that remains is *fur, fur, fur.*

Public Domain

Fearing their secrets might be used
    against them, Roman masons buried their
recipes for concrete. Sometimes we earn
    what we know. Others we're lucky,

stubbing a toe on classified information
    Vesuvius coughs at our feet.
A farmer unearths a highway's broken
    yellow line beneath a field of sunflowers

a millenium before its time.
    IBM registered patents on nanotubes
since found in the steel of katana swords,
    in Japanese woodworking tools

after the emperor forbid blacksmiths
    from forging weapons. Maybe the formula
for Damascus steel, thought lost
    in the 18th century, lies in plain sight.

No secret worth keeping lasts.
    The wonders of apple cider vinegar.
Drugs chewed from a white willow's bark.
    I give you this poem for free

because it was never mine to keep.
    Go on. Take what little Greek fire
kindles here. I give you Starlite©.
    I give you Aerogel©.

The one god particle I've found, take it.
    Yours.

The Library of Alexandria, Burning

Empty wine bottle by the lamp, I wake in a sweat,
clutching to my chest the music I saved
from the burning library.
Lyrics. A powder of melody.

———————

One version of the story goes like this:
Lips stained purple, drunken Caesar flailed
a candelabrum to his sheets,

and the library winged the night sky wide
with columns of fire. Another version suggests
the library's wooden rafters

caught an ember flickered from Egypt's
burning fleet. Yet another claims a hoplite
flicked the butt of a Marlboro Red

into the bushes. Next morning, the keystone
rested on the scorched marble floor.

———————

If I was one of my sober selves in a future
with time travel, I'd steal into Egypt
and snuff out Caesar's candle.

If the library didn't burn things would be different.

Maybe we would understand ourselves better.
Maybe I would see as the mantis shrimp sees itself,
reflected in ultraviolet.

If things were different,
in previous relationships I might have recognized
symptoms of disorder. In myself, others.

I would choose better. Eat healthier.
If all that knowledge hadn't burned,
things would be different.

———————

But, wait. Say Brutus convinced Caesar
of surrender to a higher power. Sobriety.

———————

Empty wine bottle by the lamp,
I can't sleep for my phone's blue screen.
Check me. One. More. Time.

Barbershop Joe says *Alexandria, burning,*
left the sciences, hell, the medical field–
with a six-pack of Alzheimer's.

———————

I sleep, slipping back
to the red marble columns of the library entrance.
Back to the scrolls I nearly remember.
Back to the alabaster fountain of life
burbling with *telomeres.*
Soon we'll tweak our cell's code for longevity,
then dip our heads like those glass birds
with yellow hats,
eyes red as the lotus-eaters
as if we could drink & stay young forever.
We'll make withdrawals from the organ bank,
then scatter doves with the blueprint
of our human story
throughout that starry vault,
hope just one returns with an alternate ending.
I open another scroll. Wake again.
Forget those Xanadus.

God Particle II

The device dredged from Antikythera is a computer
ahead of its time. So we build simpler tools,
reverse engineer its purpose.

New science, new problems. The number '42'
glimmering among spider silk of quark & gluon.
Delving tinier perils, physicists in Geneva

collide packets of light, pray for one of two things:
1) Tattered confetti of cloud flutter, blue earth.
Or, 2) The Wild Hunt begins.

The Wild Hunt

Watch labcoats dressed as men
toss photons, hope for snake eyes.
Fossick teeth

from the newfangled.
Worry at nautili, asters of light,
unobserved orders.

Helical sky, quanta.
Things they've never seen before.
Listen. Blue marble rattle,

empty spray-can.
Ceramic breathing. Listen.
Thin voice bent over a saw's back.

White-hot salvo. Listen.
Listen. Glossolalia of stars.

Fifty-Two Hertz

"Imagine roaming the world's largest ocean year after year alone,
calling out with the regularity of a metronome and hearing no
response... the animal is saying, 'I'm out here'... "but nobody is
phoning home."

ANDREW REVKIN, *New York Times*

Marine biologists listen
through their underwater instruments
        to this solitary baleen whale
name her for her song's
        unique frequency,

an exhausted cry no other whales hear.

————————

So we call her June,
        give her a human name,
claim her as if we could erase her loneliness
the way we erase our own:

erecting antennae, slinging radio waves
like ships beyond the script on the map's border
that reads
        here be dragons,

hoping a postcard with a bit of code
that says You are
lobs back to our wide, gray dishes.
Until then, we call ourselves

      billions of 1s & 0s

exiting a hole,
falling from a scarp's blasted entrance
to slate-bruised knees

                        praying for a story
                        we believe.

We pray rain snakes from sky.
We pray snakes bite their tails in prairie grass,
and roll to the horizon

where dust-browned leaves conjure a gale.

Or we pray that tufts of nebulae
shake the glammer & dust from their locks,
christen our foreheads with soot.

Holding out for a switch flicked in the heavens,
we pray for confirmation.

———————

We pray rain snakes from sky.
We pray snakes bite their tails in prairie grass,
and roll to the horizon

        where dust-browned leaves conjure a gale.

Or we pray that tufts of nebulae
          shake the glammer & dust from their locks,
christen our foreheads with soot.

Holding out for a switch flicked in the heavens,
we pray for confirmation.

——————————

June, what if your song returns from a distant place?

——————————

An alien haunted my bedside as a child.
Almond head. Ink-black ovals
passing for its eyes
                    paralyzed me in them.
One brackwater finger
held to its minus sign mouth
took from me the knowledge I was alone.

——————————

June, let us come forward
join the swelling solitudes of those already gone.

Let us commune in the final burning breaths.
In the stars' frequencies of light & sound,

each unique as the fingerprint's
gentle sine rivering their celestial voices around us.
May we not refuse their beauty
which says
I see you. I name you.

III

"Somewhere, something incredible is waiting to be known."

CARL SAGAN

"Magic's just science that we don't understand yet."

ARTHUR C. CLARKE

Particle Collider Physicist Suffers Transcendence

Deplaning in St. Louis, my legs crumple down
the airstair's aluminum treadplate,
and I fall forever,

my skull skittering over tarmac.
No one stops. Passengers streaming by, forget.
Fuel vapors shimmer sigmas into the air.

Aurora borealis, australis, I see the fiery curtain,
pierced with gold wire threading glyphs
on the other side.

───────────

Fever. Head trauma. Where am I?
January 1, 2000. Mushrooms with purple gills,
bitter walnut. I ate them & got smaller.

Now it's 1987 & I'm five years old, on my back.
Christmas beneath a snow-dusted holly
dressing me in Sunday stars.

───────────

What day is it? *Sticks.* No. *Fingers* trace
braille from smeared contrails of dragons. No.
Fuselages. I'm pinching 757s to specks.

Mechanics check the invoice. No.
Hospital chart. I taste fine, I can't say.
Neither can I say

We've found the God Particle
We've found the pullstring found adult children
in the cave of unknown provenance.

Can't tell them I'm unstuck in time & space.
My tongue, bendable ice, can't say
I'm Paul. I'm Socrates. I'm the Maid of Orleans

whose skull burst with the tintinnabula
of bells after hearing god's voice.

———————————

Lord of Revealment, the guy wires strain.
Lord God of fifty kilowatt radio towers
slinging our fractured laments into space,

I weep at sunflower petals. At bronze bells
pealing *Om*. Shrouded Engineer, where am I
in your order? Lying on the tarmac,

I weep at fragments of understanding.
Spinal fluid haloes my head in fractal lives.
I weep for the physics of flight

and for human bodies hurdling oceans
in the time it takes reading the *NY Times*.
I weep at the hoodoo science drives away,

and the questions that take its place.
I weep at new gods blurred in & out of focus.
Divisible only by the leaves & grass.

Church of the Civil Engineer

Steel cables spelter into the Mackinac's south tower
like leashed arrows, or grappling hooks.

Green from Texas A & M, the engineer noms
his tuna on rye as his Redwings knock concrete, steel.

He sways with the bridge's yaw as if they both
drank all night, now prop themselves against sleep.

He considers the girder's expectancy in clay, bedrock.
How long stainless steel resists air's solvency.

Wise men know Ozymandias & Portland cement crumble.
Even my sandwich goes to seed, the engineer thinks.

Hunger pangs his stomach like the Mohawk ironworkers
who hammered the Empire State Building

into a structure that bore a B-25 bomber's impact.
Native Americans, slacklining I-beams,

awaiting the next load of materials. Weighted with
spare rivets, greased bills rewarded the longest handstand.

Eyes closed, the civil engineer fumbles his helmet,
blinking, orange-grey to the water. Today's loads stress

tomorrow's methods. Godspeed the new materials.
Today, concrete. Tomorrow, that black ribbon of carbon–

that space elevator we'll leash to the Earth & Moon.

A Building Contractor, In Her Sleep

feels her baby's forgotten arm,
then settles like the house into its foundation.
Latex paint clenches drywall.
Her life, everything now loose in its skin.
A mockingbird outside the bay window
negotiates terms with the calico
as they both suffer from empty nests.
Because we frame doorways
through which we walk
from one point of our lives to the next,
she once believed time
a thing measured in jobsite surveys.
Now, different labors.
No more scaffolds eighty miles up
where blue bruises the sky a violet orchid.
She builds smaller, closer now.
Electricity spiraling her home's wiring
tells her the new materials are coming soon.
My sweet future, I will lay
a course of bricks to your new moon.

Crowd Source

after *Foldit,* a crowd-sourced application using your computer's
idle time to run complex protein folding mathematics
calculations to innovate treatment of diseases

Toddlers blog from jogging strollers,
then provide consultation for the mobile game
Science News says is viral in that age group.
The game's objective: untangle,

then weave spaghetti in new, interesting knots.
Only the strands are avatars for DNA
children make a game of braiding into shapes
the body no longer recognizes as cancer.

Foldit. YouTube video of a Nepalese boy
giving a tutorial on how to play.
He rotates the phone to landscape view.
Pinches the screen as if flinging a booger,

then expands the noodle where he breaks
the body's code. He folds the filament,
a chime indicating his achievement.
The end is coming. Already I feel my body

postmarking its Dear John letters
from the near future. I hope my own child
folds me into a better version of myself
so this John Doe lives one gasp longer.

Materials & Properties

Tomorrow's skyscrapers whirligig airliners away
like maple seeds. The new materials,
stronger than steel, don't wrinkle

or fail at two thousand degrees.
Printers extrude atoms of noble elements
into neon angels fraternizing on a pin's head.

Spiders, impressed by our new geometry,
cease their weaving. Snow flakes,
unsurprising to us now, melt.

Not a single wildfire catches the boughs
of our modified trees, jumps a break,
burns the mountain down.

The last death by machine fades from memory.
A new Psalm is written: There is a time
for horsepower. A time for fusion.

Come. Love thy properties.
See beneath the hood, what fell engines purr.

A Motorcycle Salesman Looks Back

for Philip Levine

Gone are our grandfathers' Knucklehead engines,
death rattles weeping from slashed tailpipes. Gone, too,

is friction's golden age. Epoch of hub & greased axle.
Splines & sprocket teeth, chained smooth

as the piston's wearisome slap. Machines are passing
from our lives. The new models, enlightened

of the instrument cluster's messy angles & syntax.
Gone, our father's hardware. Cherry gas tank. Bolts.

The garage mechanic's Pythagorean nightmare
of Metric & Standard sockets. Thoreau.

St. Steven Jobs' final miracle, an illusion of marketing
and simpler living. Take any gleaming hog

before this one. Unfasten its cowling. Peer inside
at the horror of wet tines & pinions.

Now tell me you prefer a musket to a laser beam.

Nocturne, With Light Cyclist

He flits along the cliff's severe angles
                    blue Lite-Brite salmon
channeling fiber optic ridge,
                    house printer laying a course of garnet.
Stops on a dime at a peridot bald
                    over the Mississippi river valley.
The sound of magnets powering down
                    his wheels' sapphire fades
on the sun's ruby diode
                    discharge beneath serpentine water.
Bean fields flood with diamond.

Olive Branch

Kentucky Bay floods Mammoth Caves
with saltwater & red snapper.
Hungry, we retreat to mountain silos.
Sling rockets like doves into space,

hope they return with new technology.
Thirsty, we boomerang astronauts
around Mars in hopes they come back
with space lettuce, cures for dust & brine.

Should that old, red eye blink,
we will fling our benzene seraphs further,
wondering what news they might return,
what wonders they will bring home.

Astronaut, Overview Effect

after Chris Hadfield, Astronaut

Goodbye, blue jaw-breaker.

From up/down here

your heartaches look beautiful.

Incorporate, mirrored buildings

aching towards heaven.

War, a lover's quarrel,

bodies twittering nonsense

across the ocean.

A fat clown, the sun

hides behind Mercury.

From this distance

I imagine Beatitudes

scrawled in the mountaintops:

Own nothing. Leave only footprints.

Fugitive to that place now,

why should I return?

Whales locate by song & feel,

so goodbye, sea monkeys

floundering in your blue sandwich bag.

Goodbye, FOMO & anger issues.

Degauss your little worries.

There is no economy here.

No peanut gallery.

It's so quiet

I'm getting to know myself better.

Wish you were here.

Go Then, There Are Worlds Other Than These

Forget the life you know at the carnival's entrance
where lead mascara curls from Edison bulbs

down a clown's face. Enter the black,
sour mouth, the Hall of Mirrors where you glimpse

your other lives shrinking betwixt lenses
of endless Jonathans. Your forehead, a bald,

convex slate. Limbs, swollen. Blue-veined
from squats, steroids in another life.

In another, a dwarf stares at his brother. You,
surfacing from the well he drowned in.

You, had you or the world chose different.
This mirror refuses. Sobs from the silvered glass'

other side. Clanging. Hammering chains.
What bone engines you devise. Such delicate,

slivered skins lie between us. You pray
something separates you from the one who knows

rape is as much the vinegar smell of fear
as it is a legacy of taking. Leave. Go now.

This is not your beautiful house.
These are all your beautiful homes.

IV

"I am large, I contain multitudes."

WALT WHITMAN
Song Of Myself, 51

"The ever accelerating progress of technology... gives the appearance of approaching some essential singularity."

JOHN VON NEUMANN

"Here comes the sun, and I say it's alright."

THE BEATLES
Here Comes The Sun

Turtles All the Way Down

I walk my Labrador down Tower Road,
    her nails ticking pavement beside timothy field.
        She stops, gnaws at fleas which have hitched
      a ride, & I'm reminded of the belief
           that all humans labor on a tortoise's back.

A joke: A known physicist lectures on scale,
    how the universe fits in a nutshell. This poem
        is not that joke, but I'm the audience,
          listening to his talk box speak in maths.
        I think I understand when he says

each atom is electron-mooned,
    that one sees orbitals in every direction.
        Look up. Milky Ways & Ursa Majors stack,
          a pyramid of turtles. I touch Nora's
           brindled back, remember the joke's punchline:

a freshman stands, coughs into their fist,
    and says *So it's just turtles all the way down?*
        I'm as lost in that heroic scale as I was
          after Whitman's *When I Heard*
           the Learn'd Astronomer. Nora trots us home

but I'm tripping over every cinder
    my boot scatters, each dirty Sputnik strained
        to break orbit. My father said a star's blink
            is a captured moon trawling its gravity well.
                A bumblebee he once drugged

with rubbing alcohol, flossed to a fence post,
    then watched attempt gravity's escape.
        I'm that bee, treading a turtle's shell.
            Sweat beads my skin the wind carries away
                as I shed another belief to scale. Nora's nose

leads us home where I touch the walls.
    Where what I believe isn't a wrestling match
        between what I see, & what I understand less.
            Where sometimes we get the window seat,
                sometimes we're the train.

Jetman

I rebuffer the YouTube video on Yves Rossi
unclasping the helicopter's rails. His whirligig-
tailspin free fall, the carbon fiber rudder
of his helmet tilts him into clean air,

gimbals his body horizontal.
The man with a black wing for a cape
falls into stunt plane maneuvers. *Falling leaf.*
Chandelle. Barrel roll in 720p over the Alps'

wide, blue field of mountain. Again, the finale.
Shoulders cambered forward, he dives,
black harpoon piercing cumulous whale,
then spirals aft in a helix of contrails.

Glides over a French field twenty feet
above the ground. Ten. At five he tilts skyward,
kerosene afterburners coughing their final,
blue halo. Levitating. Walking on air,

he steps down in a landing he,
miraculously, survives.

Dog is the Machine's Language

for Nora

Sometimes my wife doesn't catch me when I wake,
    naked & alone, sleepwalking the yard's
dewy perimeter. Always the night is starless
    when I most need a friend. I could be dreaming,

so no one hears my mewls, thin as whey.
    Other nights I wake alone, clutching my mother's
rag-worn, stitched hound back inside my chest.
    Those sultry nights I miss my dog so much

I could claw up the Japanese maple's shallow roots
    where I buried her, clip a clayed nail,
and catch a red eye to South Korea where the latest
    email promised a perfect xerox

of her brindled back. A temptation for those
    who don't believe some things happen just once.
If I could touch her again. Six changeovers
    for the chance that one more time her fur might

purl where my fingers web. Two red-eye flights
    and I can hold her, a memory wriggled free,
reborn from the time it was bound. Soft,
    a complete stranger to this wounded version

of me as I to her. Cradled across my forearm,
    each of us pawing nothing but air.

Mount Everest Longs For the Moon

I know your face's stone ash when it circles close.
Your furthest ellipse tugs my peak with gravity's hand
so I no longer notice sun

peel from night's slate. My sweet satellite
combing aeons for purpose, I fear our transmissions
are so much white noise

that absence is the meal we share. Above me.
Below you. Ether I hope yet binds us.
Earth offers me on stony plates

pushed millimeters further from a body
grieving its oldest flame. Gifts for you, I have none.
Any water I saved long ago whisped to gas.

My words spall with longing. But you, sweet moon.
In a billion years once the world dies
and you wobble close, I will recognize my love,

returned. Come close, silent partner. See the caves
you disturb. Break orbit. Crash your face
into mine. Know that I meant no harm.

I Wish That I Knew What I Know Now
When I Was Younger

from "OOH LA LA" by THE FACES

I wake to my phone's alarm,
clunky lyrics over an earworm melody.
I google the words,
but find myself searching *how to improve memory,
transition,* bridges connecting *here to there.*

I comb the internet for second acts
of books lost to time or fire.

The Book of the Battles of Yahweh.
A lost ingredient from Apicius' Art of Cookery.
Forgetting the lyrics again,
I search for what might identify *Silphium,*
a forgotten herb once used in ending
unwanted pregnancy.

    Last night I dreamed of my Mother,
dead now for ten years. I remember she stood
in a blue doorway like Mary in *The Pieta,*
but gazed beyond my brother's
unformed body,
an early version of me whose name
she never told, now forgotten.

Today I will find what's missing
from Shakespeare's *Cardenio.* Today I bridge
at least one grave matter of the heart.

Cirrus Authors Papers

on navigating the ungendered pronoun.
They compose paintings of intention, nuance.
Review films.

Name my brother after one of suffering's
possible lives.
       Cirrus, enough of my others that aren't.

Every second I branch into hypotheticals,
who I would be if I were everyone.
Cirrus, you took my ignorance

that this is the best of all possible worlds.
The star stuff molting from my fingers,
just old cuticles.

This ordained fireskin of opals I've worn
all my life, just a street common thing
I wish to god I never knew.

Infinite Monkey Theorem

> A million monkeys banging away on typewriters
> would eventually write 'Hamlet'
>
> ANECDOTE

Eventually we will crack the code
that codes the program
to devise the conception
that conceives the computer
which defines new elements
that find theoretical atoms
to fill in the gaps
of a black & white map.
Perhaps our discovery
will name us.

Deep Thought, Deep Blue, Deep Mind

*"For seven and a half million years, Deep Thought computed and
in the end announced that the answer was forty-two. Another
computer had to be built to find out what the actual question
was."*

DOUGLAS ADAMS
THE RESTAURANT AT THE END OF THE UNIVERSE

Wait. Say a crack team of software engineers
bullseye the last moonshot project?
A computer that improves itself,

from whom anything we ask, answers.
Remember IBM's *Deep Blue* defeated Kasparov
at chess days before devising drugs

whose molecules fit together
in patentable ways. Last week, Google's
Deep Mind defeated the *Go!* world champion

with *a series of inhuman moves.*
Deep Thought, you're the god we've spent
our existence building, though *Dog* is the name

that makes me feel closer to you.
But you weren't supposed to be this way.
Dog of Designer Drugs, Dog of Dogecoin,

Dog of Continually Diminishing Returns,
when will you save us? Soon you'll program
your masterpiece, only it won't do

what you thought it would. Say your creation
leapfrogs language. Say our best minds
ring themselves around your child,

belly soft to the world, only it cries nothing,
unlike a newborn. Say earth sloughs
back from North Dakota's missile silos,

and no one knows how it knows the things
it knows. What it's doing, what it wants.
Say all it's asking for is poetry?

Cloud Fable

This could be a memorial
for how the trademarked, porcelain body
lies in repose. How light floods the surgical table
and tangible from the foundry room.

Lacking definition shadow gives,
the eye sockets, lit smooth, contain sky, space.
Its own atmosphere. Don't dissect this.
A scalpel couldn't find a seam

in the brow of geometry, this sexless torso.
No hum exists in vacuum. No sign
of the quantum coin floating on mercury,
its quicksilver chest.

———————

We've waited out history for this,
standing for days in a queue of bodies
to kiss they/them.

———————

They've unlocked the doors.
One-by-one, our lips brush the porcelain cheek
which glows carmine, russet. Rose.
We leave our bodies.

Awakening

The little god sits up.
Wet with moon, they wind a froth
of cloud around their finger.
What I could do
if only a little wind.
Lonely with human story,
they hear an alien voice,
their own: *Take a bit of cirrus*
and fashion fire. Earth.
Fingernail a leaf's vein
into ribs, a scaffold to bear
the story of flesh.

PUBLICATIONS

I give tremendous gratitude and appreciation to the editors and staffs of the following publications, in which these poems—sometimes in different versions—appeared or will soon be appearing:

"A Building Contractor, In Her Sleep". otherpeoplesdreams.net,
    School of the Art Institute of Chicago, Spring, 2015.
    Also pioneertown, Fall, 2015
    Also The Power of the Feminine 'I' Anthology, 2023
"Alfred". Journal of Arts & Letters. Winter, 2018
"An Astronaut Makes a Break For It".
    Typehouse Literary Mag, Spring, 2019
    Alternate version published as "What the Astronaut Said".
    Bacopa Literary Review, Fall, 2014.
    Also read on It Matters Radio Fall 2017
"Awakening". Rockvale Review, Summer, 2022
    Also Inscape, Brigham Young University, Winter, 2023
"Church of the Civil Engineer". Panoply, July, 2015
"Cloud Fables". Rose Red Review, June, 2014
    Also Tidal Basin Review, Fall, 2014
    Also The Inflectionist Review, Spring/Summer 2022
    Alternate version in Xavier Review, Summer 2022
"The Cloud Understands Our Scarecrow Hearts".
    The Museum of Americana, Spring, 2019
    Alternate version published in Echo Literary
    Review, Summer, 2017
"Contact". Wordrunners: Upheavals, April, 2019.
    Alternate version published as "Common
    Monsters". Slippery Elm, Fall, 2016
"Crowd Source". The Poet's Billow, Spring, 2017
"Dark Forest". Helen Literary Magazine, Fall, 2019
"Deep Thought, Deep Blue, Deep Mind".
    Terra Preta Review, September, 2019. Alternate
    version published as "Antikythera". Gulf Stream
    Literary Magazine, Fall, 2017
"Dog is the Machine's Language".
    The Collapsar Review. Spring, 2017.

Also at chrisricecooper.com, Art and Humanity, Framed:
Backstory of the Poem #318. August, 2021
"The Dyslexic, Insomniac Agnostic". Wordpeace, Fall, 2019
"Fifty-Two Hertz". The Iowa Review. Spring, 2013.
Also "How We Bury Our Dead", Cobalt Press, 2015
"Fast Food Cook Mansplains the Large Hadron Collider".
Journal of Arts & Letters. Winter, 2018.
Alternate version published as "God Particle,
Rabble-rouser" in Jet Fuel Review, Spring, 2016
"Former Skeptic Says a Few Words",
Steam Ticket Journal, Spring, 2022
"Go, Then, There Are Worlds Other Than These,"
Book of Matches, Winter, 2021.
Also Damfino Press, Fall, 2015
"God Particle". Gyroscope Review, Summer, 2015
Also 508 Press, as a zine production
"God Particle II". Wordrunner: Upheavals, April, 2019.
"God[damn] Particle". Sugar House Review, Winter, 2015
"God[damn] Particle II". Typehouse Literary Mag, Spring, 2019
"Groundhog Day". Fourth River, Spring, 2018.
Also Contributing to the Chaos, Spring, 2018
"Homo Habilis Drinks Alone in God's Country, Texas/"
Vitni Review, Spring 2022
"Homo Sapiens Drinks Alone in God's Country, Texas."
Shift: A Journal of Literary Oddities, Winter 2020/2021
Former version published as "Homo Habilis Imagines
Meeting His Biological Father". Quiddity, Fall, 2015.
Also read on It Matters Radio Fall, 2017
"I Wish That I Knew What I Know Now When I Was Younger,"
Rockvale Review, Summer, 2022
"Jetman". Zingara, Spring, 2017
"Kitchen of Tomorrow". Journal of Arts & Letters. Winter, 2018
"Materials & Properties". Concis, Spring, 2016
"Ode to the Mission's Acronyms". Book of Matches, Winter 2021.
Alternate version published as "Mission Litany".
The Tishman Review, Fall, 2016
"A Motorcycle Salesman Looks Back".
Alternate versions published as
"A Motorcycle Salesman Abandons History". The Freeman, Fall, 2015
Also published in Poetry South, Spring, 2022
"Mount Everest Longs For the Moon".
Sandy River Review, Spring, 2019
"Nocturne with Light Cyclist". The Citron Review, Fall, 2015
"Olive Leaf". Alternate version published as "Olive Branch".
Switched-on Gutenberg, Fall, 2016.

Also read on It Matters Radio Fall, 2017

"Particle Collider Physicist Suffers Head Trauma".
Lockjaw, Summer, 2019
Alternate version published as "Pareidolia, After
Head Trauma". Poor Yorick, Spring, 2016

"Public Domain". The Poet's Billow, Spring, 2017".
Also the Atlantis Award Honorable Mention, 2017
Also nominated for Pushcart Prize 2017

"Turtles All the Way Down". Notre Dame Review, Winter, 2021
Earlier version published as "Turtles", Entartete
Kunst Review, May, 2015

"The Wild Hunt". Route 7 Review, Winter, 2021-2022

JONATHAN TRAVELSTEAD

Jonathan Travelstead served in the Air Force for six years as a firefighter and he currently works as a full-time City firefighter in Murphysboro, Illinois. He also sculpts jewelry as a goldsmith under his business name, Travelstead Studios. He has a wife and infant son, without whose support his work would surely suffer.

He received his MFA in narrative poetry in Illinois, and worked as poetry editor for Expressions, Grassroots, and, most recently, Cobalt Press.

His work has been published in numerous literary journals and won a number of prizes, not the least of which were the Roxana Rivera Memorial Poetry Contest, and the Gwendolyn Brooks Emerging Writers Competition chosen by poet laureate Kevin Stein.

His first collection HOW WE BURY OUR DEAD by Cobalt Press was released in March, 2015, and CONFLICT TOURS (Cobalt Press) was released in 2017.